Celebrate

INDEPENDENCE
DAY

BY Barbara deRubertis

The Kane Press
New York

For activities and resources for this book and
others in the HOLIDAYS & HEROES series, visit:
www.kanepress.com/holidays-and-heroes

Text copyright © 2016 by Barbara deRubertis
Photographs/images copyrights: Cover: © franckreporter/iStock; pages 1, 29 top: © wavebreakmedia/
Shutterstock.com; page 3 top: © Geoffrey Kuchera/Shutterstock.com; page 3 bottom: © Joseph Sohm/
Shutterstock.com; pages 4, 5, & 6 © North Wind Picture Archives -- All rights reserved; page 7 top: © Ken
Brown/iStock; page 7 bottom: © North Wind Picture Archives -- All rights reserved; page 8: Library of
Congress, Prints & Photographs Division, LC-USZC2-2243; page 9 left: © North Wind Picture Archives --
All rights reserved; page 9 right: Library of Congress, Manuscript Division; page 10: © Victorian Traditions/
Shutterstock.com; page 11: The White House Historical Association (White House Collection); pages 12–13:
US Capitol; page 14 top: © Everett Historical/Shutterstock.com; page 14 bottom left: © Tatiana Belova/
iStock; page 14 bottom right: © Everett Historical/Shutterstock.com; page 15 top: © North Wind Picture
Archives -- All rights reserved; page 15 bottom: © Mark R/Shutterstock.com; pages 16, 17: © North Wind
Picture Archives -- All rights reserved; page 18 top: Library of Congress, Prints & Photographs Division,
LC-DIG-highsm-15716; page 18 bottom: © Susan Law Cain/Shutterstock.com; page 19: Architect of the
Capitol; page 20: © javarman/Shutterstock.com; page 20 inset: © David Smart/Shutterstock.com; page
21 left: The White House Historical Association; page 21 right: US Navy Photo; pages 22, 23, 24, 25: ©
North Wind Picture Archives -- All rights reserved; page 26 top: © Joseph Sohm/Shutterstock.com; page 26
middle: © Cory A Ulrich/Shutterstock.com; page 26 bottom: © cdrin/Shutterstock.com; page 27 top: © Susan
Chiang/iStock; page 27 bottom left: © JMichl/iStock; page 27 bottom right: © ktaylorg/iStock; page 28 top: ©
Valentina Proskurina/Shutterstock.com; page 28 bottom: © The Blade/Amy E. Voigt; page 29 bottom: © Jani
Bryson/iStock; page 30: © MivPiv/iStock; page 31: © Steve Heap/Shutterstock.com; page 32: © M_a_y_a/
iStock
All due diligence has been conducted in identifying copyright holders and obtaining permissions.

Library of Congress Cataloging-in-Publication Data

deRubertis, Barbara author.
Let's celebrate Independence Day / by Barbara deRubertis.
    pages cm. -- (Holidays & heroes)
  Audience: Ages 6-10.
  ISBN 978-1-57565-830-8 (library reinforced binding : alk. paper) -- ISBN 978-1-57565-747-9 (pbk. :
alk. paper)
 1. Fourth of July--Juvenile literature. 2. Fourth of July celebrations--Juvenile literature. I. Title.
  E286.A1268 2016
  394.2634--dc23
                                    2015028191

eISBN: 978-1-57565-748-6

1 2 3 4 5 6 7 8 9 10

First published in the United States of America in 2016 by Kane Press, Inc.
Printed in the United States of America

Book Design: Edward Miller
Photograph/Image Research: Poyee Oster

Visit us online at **www.kanepress.com**.

Like us on Facebook
facebook.com/kanepress

Follow us on Twitter
@KanePress

When we think of the Fourth of July, we think of fireworks, flags, parades, and picnics. America has been celebrating Independence Day with gusto since July 4, 1776. It is one of our country's most important national holidays!

But what are the reasons for all this excitement?

To get the whole story, we have to go back to the years *before* American independence.

In 1773, the 13 American colonies belonged to Great Britain and were ruled by King George III. But people living in these colonies were unhappy. Why? They were not being treated fairly!

Angry colonists in Boston, Massachusetts, protest high taxes.

The dumping of British tea in Boston's harbor became known as The Boston Tea Party!

One big problem was that colonists were being asked to pay more and more taxes to the British government on basic things like sugar and tea. And they had no say in the matter whatsoever.

So the colonists resisted paying the taxes. Some even protested by dumping a shipment of British tea into the waters of Boston's harbor! The British government passed harsh laws to punish the colonists.

British "redcoats" entered the towns of Lexington and Concord, Massachusetts, on April 19, 1775, and were met by local militiamen. The first shots of the war were fired.

In 1774, delegates from the 13 colonies gathered in Philadelphia for the First Continental Congress, which would now act as the colonists' own government. The delegates asked the colonists to refuse to buy British goods because of the high taxes.

In April of 1775, fighting broke out between the American colonists and the British soldiers. This marked the beginning of the American Revolutionary War.

In May, delegates to a Second Continental Congress met in Philadelphia. They sent a letter directly to King George asking him to protect the colonists and their interests. He refused even to read their letter!

By January of 1776, there was much debate in the colonies about whether or not they should separate themselves from Great Britain. More and more, the colonists disliked the idea of being ruled by a king.

King George III

GEORGE III
1760-1820

76

The Second Continental Congress met at the State House in Philadelphia, Pennsylvania. The building was later renamed Independence Hall.

By June of 1776, the Second Continental Congress was ready to take a bold step. They would prepare a document declaring their independence from Great Britain.

A "Committee of Five" was appointed to draft the document. The committee decided that Thomas Jefferson should write the first draft.

The Committee of Five (from left to right: Thomas Jefferson, Roger Sherman, Benjamin Franklin, Robert R. Livingston, and John Adams)

Thomas Jefferson reads his draft to Benjamin Franklin.

Jefferson's rough draft, June 1776

Jefferson was not a great speaker, but he was an excellent writer. He sat down at a desk in the Philadelphia boarding house where he was staying and began to write. He tried to express the basic desires of the American colonists for a fair government. Then he described 27 ways they were not being treated fairly by the king. He wrote from his heart.

His draft was presented to the Congress on June 28.

Benjamin Franklin, John Adams, and Thomas Jefferson work on a draft of the Declaration of Independence.

For two days, members of the Congress worked on the draft. They shortened it, removed unnecessary words, and rewrote sentences.

After a long day of speeches and debate on July 1, it was time to vote on whether or not to declare independence from Great Britain. There were several delegates from each colony, but each colony had only one vote.

Nine of the thirteen colonies voted yes. Pennsylvania and South Carolina voted no, Delaware's vote was a tie, and New York did not vote.

The delegates decided to vote again the next day. They hoped to be "united" in their vote for independence.

Delegates debate the Declaration of Independence.

On July 2, 1776, the delegates voted a second time. Two delegates from Pennsylvania who had voted no chose not to vote, which changed that colony's vote to yes. South Carolina's delegates changed their vote from no to yes. A delegate from Delaware arrived after an all-night ride and voted yes, breaking the tie.

So this time, delegates from 12 of the 13 colonies voted in favor of independence!

New York's delegates still did not vote . . . but they voted in favor of independence a week later. This made the vote unanimous!

From this day on, the American colonies would be known as the United States of America. It had declared itself to be an independent nation.

Presenting the declaration

On July 3, John Adams wrote a letter to his wife predicting that July 2 would become the most important American holiday. He said the day should be celebrated *"with pomp and parade, with shows, games, sports, guns, bells, bonfires, and illuminations, from one end of this continent to the other, from this time forward forever more."*

John Adams

Abigail Adams

Delegates sign the Declaration of Independence.

But it was on July 4 that the final wording of the Declaration of Independence was approved by a vote of the Congress, which made it official. This hand-written copy, dated July 4, 1776, was signed with a flourish by John Hancock, President of the Congress. So instead of July 2, July 4 became the most important American holiday!

Reading the Declaration of Independence to a cheering crowd in Philadelphia, 1776

During the night of July 4, two hundred copies of the Declaration were printed. They were distributed throughout the states and were sent to other nations. The United States of America was introducing itself to the world!

On July 6, a newspaper in Philadelphia was the first to publish the Declaration of Independence. And two days later, the Declaration was read in public for the first time—with music playing and bells ringing.

A copy was also given to George Washington, Commander of the Continental Army, who had it read to his troops. He hoped it would inspire them in their fight against the British.

George Washington leading the Continental Army

On July 19,
Congress ordered
an "official" copy of
the Declaration of
Independence, hand-
written on parchment.
On August 2, it
was signed by 56 delegates to the Second
Continental Congress. This official copy is
now displayed in the Rotunda of the National
Archives Building in Washington, D.C.

After the Declaration of Independence was signed, the Revolutionary War continued for five more years. The British finally surrendered in 1781. A peace treaty between the Americans and the British was signed in 1783.

The British surrender

Why is this Declaration so important?

The preamble to the Declaration of Independence is famous because it spells out, in simple language, what should be the basic rights of all people, everywhere:

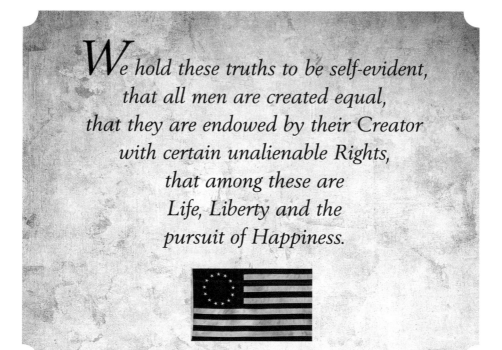

We hold these truths to be self-evident, that all men are created equal, that they are endowed by their Creator with certain unalienable Rights, that among these are Life, Liberty and the pursuit of Happiness.

The preamble set the stage for a new kind of government—unlike any other the world had seen. In this new government, the people would rule themselves!

An interesting coincidence . . .

July 4, 1826, was the 50th anniversary of the Declaration of Independence. Both John Adams and Thomas Jefferson had signed the Declaration, both had later served as President of the United States, and both died on this exact day!

Thomas Jefferson

John Adams

How did Independence Day become a holiday?

Before the Revolutionary War, the birthday of King George III was celebrated in the American colonies with parades, speeches, bonfires, and the ringing of bells.

During the summer of 1776, after the Declaration of Independence was signed, some Americans held mock funerals for King George! This was their way of celebrating their freedom from his rule.

Americans tear down the statue of George III in New York City to celebrate independence, 1776.

Also during that summer, special festivities marked the first public readings of the Declaration of Independence throughout the states. There were parades, concerts, and bonfires . . . and cannons and muskets were fired!

Americans celebrate news of the Declaration of Independence, 1776.

Washington's soldiers raise the 13-star American flag.

The first annual celebration of Independence Day was held in Philadelphia on July 4, 1777, while the Revolutionary War was still being fought. On July 4, 1778, George Washington gave his soldiers a double ration of rum to celebrate the day! In the 1800s, Independence Day celebrations became more and more popular. And in 1870, Congress made the Fourth of July a national holiday.

The 100th anniversary of the Fourth of July is celebrated in front of Independence Hall in Philadelphia in 1876.

How do Americans celebrate Independence Day now?

Many people fly American flags at their homes on Independence Day, and many businesses are closed. The day is celebrated with parades, concerts, speeches, festivals, and patriotic ceremonies.

People also have picnics, block parties, ice cream socials, sporting events, contests, and family reunions. They often decorate their parties, food, and even themselves with red, white, and blue.

And as soon as it gets dark, many cities provide *dramatic* firework displays!

At most Independence Day celebrations, people join together to sing America's national anthem, "The Star-Spangled Banner." People also recite the Pledge of Allegiance to the American flag.

"The Star-Spangled Banner"
O say can you see, by the dawn's early light,
What so proudly we hailed at the twilight's last gleaming,
Whose broad stripes and bright stars through the perilous fight,
O'er the ramparts we watched, were so gallantly streaming?
And the rockets' red glare, the bombs bursting in air,
Gave proof through the night that our flag was still there;
O say does that star-spangled banner yet wave
O'er the land of the free and the home of the brave?

Francis Scott Key wrote the poem that was used as the words for "The Star-Spangled Banner" in 1814 (during the War of 1812). It became our national anthem in 1931.

The Pledge of Allegiance
"I pledge allegiance to the Flag
of the United States of America,
and to the Republic for which it stands,
one Nation under God, indivisible,
with liberty and justice for all."

Francis Bellamy composed the words to the Pledge of Allegiance in 1892. A few changes were made before it was adopted by Congress in 1942. The words "under God" were added in 1954.

Wherever Americans are in the world, when July 4 rolls around they usually celebrate Independence Day. Members of our armed forces who are stationed outside the United States celebrate if they possibly can. American embassies in foreign countries host parties. And groups of Americans gather privately to celebrate the treasured freedoms we enjoy.

In Washington, D.C., a free concert is performed on the Capitol building's lawn every year, and it attracts over half a million people. Called "A Capitol Fourth," it is broadcast live across America and to our armed service members in other parts of the world. The concert is followed by a spectacular firework display.

It is our great privilege to live in the United States of America, "the land of the free . . . and the home of the brave." Many Americans have given their lives over the years defending our ideals and our freedoms. We can show our gratitude by respecting these freedoms and using them wisely, by being good citizens, and by treating all our fellow human beings with respect.

This nation will remain the land of the free only so long as it is the home of the brave.
—Elmer Davis, American journalist